TITANIC

THE COOKBOOK

RECIPES FROM THE ERA OF THE GREAT OCEAN LINERS

YVONNE HUME
ELAINE ELLIOT AND VIRGINIA LEE

FORMAC PUBLISHING COMPANY LIMITED
HALIFAX

Formac Publishing Company Limited recognizes the support of the Province of Nova Scotia through the Department of Communities, Culture and Heritage. We are pleased to work in partnership with the Culture Division to develop and promote our cultural resources for all Nova Scotians. We acknowledge the financial support of the Government of Canada through the Canada Book Fund for our publishing activities.

Cover Photo Credits:
Front cover top: Nova Scotia Archives
Front cover bottom: Jen Partridge
Back cover top left: istock photography
Backc cover top right, bottom: Jen partridge

Library and Archives Canada Cataloguing in Publication

Hume, Yvonne, 1954-
        Titanic : the cookbook : recipes from the era of the great
ocean liners / Yvonne Hume, Elaine Elliot, Virginia Lee.

Includes index.
Issued also in electronic formats.
ISBN 978-1-4595-0111-9

        1. Titanic (Steamship). 2. Cooking. 3. Cookbooks.
I. Elliot, Elaine, 1939- II. Lee, Virginia, 1947- III. Title.

TX652.H855 2012   641.5   C2012-902890-8

Formac Publishing Company Limited
5502 Atlantic Street
Halifax, Nova Scotia, Canada
B3H 1G4
www.formac.ca

Printed and bound in Hong Kong.

CONTENTS

INTRODUCTION

★

PREFACE

Yvonne Hume

WHEN I FIRST DECIDED TO WRITE a cookery book based on menus served on the *Titanic*, I had no idea what a huge undertaking and responsibility it would be. I began to realize that many people wanted a *Titanic* cookery book that was easy to use, but still authentic and true to the ship. First I had to locate the original menus; I then had to research what each individual recipe consisted of, down to the smallest ingredients. Many of the recipes I already knew due to the fact that I have many years of catering experience and have cooked in my own restaurants in the past. Regarding the ones I was not familiar with: I gathered a huge array of information from top chefs and uncovered the common theme of ingredients in each dish, fully allowing that each chef puts his own mark on a recipe. I used my cookery skills and developed the recipe ingredients list and cooking instructions to produce an authentic dish that would be workable for cooks of all skill levels. We have cooking styles today that differ greatly from those used one hundred years ago, so as far as presentation is concerned, use your own flair to present your meal in a way that is individual to you. I hope you enjoy indulging in the food from this wonderful era.

INTRODUCTION

Elaine Elliot and Virginia Lee

WE WERE DELIGHTED TO BE INVITED to adapt the recipes in the British edition of this book to reflect North American ingredients and measurements. As Nova Scotians, the *Titanic* is a part of our heritage and an intriguing chapter of our maritime history.

The *Titanic* was built to be the greatest ocean liner of the early twentieth century. She attracted the rich and famous as well as those seeking a better life in the new world. Her first-class passengers were treated to the finest of foods. Second- and third-class passengers no doubt expected less, but menus indicate they were served typical British fare.

We invite you to imagine that you too are onboard the *Titanic*. Polish the silver, shine the crystal and bring out your finest china. Plan a menu as it would have been served in first class, offering several courses, perhaps including Duck Liver Pâté with Toast Points, followed by Rice Soup, Filet Mignon Lili and decadent Chocolate Ganache Eclairs. Be sure to include a course of fresh fruit and a cheese tray. Sound too difficult? Picture your guests as Irish immigrants, munching on Cabin Biscuits and enjoying a Lamb Stew. Whatever your cooking skills, we are sure there will be dining options in the recipes offered in this book. Bon appétit!

THE TITANIC

Yvonne Hume

ON WEDNESDAY APRIL 10, 1912 the port of Southampton was a hive of activity. Boat trains began arriving in rapid succession early in the morning, beginning with second- and third-class passengers. Trains carrying the cream of Edwardian society were pulling up alongside the ship until just thirty minutes before its departure at noon. The embarking passengers were greeted by musicians, a trio and a quintet, who played a variety of tunes that were mainly uptempo. The *Titanic* set sail from the quayside carnival atmosphere and arrived in Cherbourg at 6:35 p.m. for a few cross-channel passengers to disembark and more transatlantic passengers to board. How exciting it must have been for those passengers to board this wonderful, "unsinkable" ship. I know the thrill and expectation that I have felt when boarding luxury liners. On one occasion I sailed across the Atlantic to New York on the *QE2*. On the third day we encountered force nine gales; to feel so helpless and at the mercy of the elements was very frightening. I remember thinking at the time how dreadful it must have been for the passengers and crew on the *Titanic*.

At 8:10 p.m. the *Titanic* set sail from Cherbourg for Queenstown, Ireland, where she arrived the next morning at half past eleven. This was to be the *Titanic*'s last port of call. More passengers were taken on, mainly steerage travellers who were setting off for a new life in America. At 1:30 p.m. the *Titanic* set sail again, this time for New York City.

At 11:40 p.m. on April 14, 1912 the *Titanic* hit an iceberg that ripped a 100-metre gash in her starboard side. By 2:20 a.m. on April 15, the ship had completely sunk.

Out of 2,207 passengers and crew, only 706 survived.

SETTING THE SCENE

★

HOW TO SET THE SCENE

WHEN YOU THROW A TITANIC PARTY, it's a great opportunity to dust off the old china, polish the family silver and celebrate with style. White table linens are a must, and remember, you can never have too many candles. Use some of the napkin folding techniques in the following section. Set the mood with fresh flowers, especially orchids and roses, which allude to wealth and glamour. Print a menu for each guest and use place cards for seating assignments.

Let your home resemble a fine liner. While few of us have a grand staircase like *Titanic*, you could put planks over the front steps to create a gangplank or post a "First Class" sign on the entrance door. Request that guests dress for the occasion — black tie for gentlemen and gowns for ladies.

INVITATIONS

PRINT YOUR OWN INVITATIONS and send them out well in advance to give your guests time to prepare. You might want to include some links about the *Titanic* or a sheet of *Titanic* facts and expectations regarding dress code and so on. We have provided an invitation template that can be photocopied and personalized.

WHITE STAR LINE

BOARDING PASS

PERMISSION GRANTED TO COME ABOARD

WHITE STAR LINE'S

R.M.S.

TITANIC

_____

_____

WHITE STAR LINE   TICKET # 4512

Passenger Ticket per Steamship: R.M.S. *Titanic*

SAILING FROM: Southhampton   DATE: 10/c April 1912

PASSENGER NAME: Mrs. Emma Eliza Bucknell

AGE: 32   FROM: Boston, Massachusetts

ACCOMPANIED BY: Mr. Alfred Bucknell (husband)

CLASS: 1ST [X] 2ND [ ] 3RD [ ]   CABIN # D-18

TRAVELLING TO: Boston, Massachusetts

REASON: Returning from a holiday in Europe with her husband, who was combining a vacation and business trip.

PASSENGER FACT: The couple is travelling with their niece Miss Kornelia Theodosia.

WHITE STAR LINE

BOARDING PASS

PERMISSION GRANTED TO COME ABOARD

WHITE STAR LINE'S

R.M.S.

TITANIC

WHITE STAR LINE

TICKET #

Passenger Ticket per Steamship: R.M.S. *Titanic*

SAILING FROM: .... DATE: *10th April* 19*12*

PASSENGER NAME: ....

AGE: .... FROM: ....

ACCOMPANIED BY: ....

CLASS: 1ST ☐ 2ND ☐ 3RD ☐ CABIN # ....

TRAVELLING TO: ....

REASON: ....

....

....

PASSENGER FACT: ....

....

....

....

WHAT TO WEAR

WHILE MALE EVENING DRESS has changed little from the time of the *Titanic*, women primarily wore floor length evening gowns. As you prepare your gala *Titanic* dinner, pull out all the stops and dress to the nines. Bling, bling and more bling will be the order of the day.

WHAT TO LISTEN TO

ON THE TITANIC, there were two musical ensembles: a five-piece orchestra and a string trio. The repertotire ran the gamut from grand opera and light or comic opera to more popular songs and waltzes. The musicicans were also familiar with the jazz rhythms of American Ragtime. Below is a selection of CDs that feature music played on board.

Titanic (4-CD Collector's Anniversary Edition) by James Horner and Celine Dion (1997)

Music Aboard the Titanic by Carol Wolfe, Nat D. Ayer, Irving Berlin, Franz Lehar and Ignace Jan Paderewski (1998)

Music From the Titanic: 21 Authentic Songs From the Epic Journey by Mary Jane Newman and Southampton Pier Players (1998)

And The Band Played On: Music Played on the Titanic by Robert Vollstedt, Sydney Baynes, John Philip Sousa, Pyotr Il'yich Tchaikovsky and Percy Grainger (2012)

Titanic: Music as Heard on the Fateful Voyage by Ian Whitcomb (1997)

WHAT TO DRINK

TO MAKE THE EXPERIENCE TRULY AUTHENTIC for your guests, use this list
of wines, spirits and liqueurs from the *Titanic* to create your drinks menu.

Champagne
Cliquot 1900; Pommeroy Naturel 1900;
Moet & Chandon, Dry Imperial 1898;
Heidsieck, Dry Monopole 1898, 1900;
Mumm's G. H., Extra Dry 1900; Perrier
Jouet, Extra Quality, Extra Dry 1898;
Ruinart, Vin Brut

Claret
Chateau Camponac; Medoc; Chateau
Rauzan Segla, First Quality

Sauterne
Sauterne

Hock Rhine wine
Nonpareli, sparkling; Rudesheim, still

Moselle
Nonpareli, sparkling; Josephshofer, still

Port
Old Matured; Fine Old Tawny

Sherry
Vino de Pasto

Burgundy
Volnay

Vermouth
French; Italian

Rum
Jamaican

Gin
Geneva; Warrington; Old Tom

Brandy
Hennesy; Martell; Frapin;
Liquer, Hine; Liquer, Frapin

Whiskey
Irish, John Jameson & Sons (ten-year-old);
Scotch, Canadian Club, Hannis (eleven-
year-old)

Liqueurs
Crème de Menthe; Benedictine;
Chartreuse (yellow); Chartreuse (green);
Curacao; Kummel

NAPKIN FOLDING

OPEN FAN NAPKIN

1 Start with a flat square napkin and fold the left-hand side over to the right.

4 Fold the unpleated part of the napkin into a triangle.

2 From the bottom of the napkin; start to fold the halved napkin in a concertina pleat, leaving one third of the napkin unpleated.

5 Stand the napkin up along the edge of the triangle pleat.

3 Carefully turn the napkin over, making sure that you hold the pleats tight, and then fold the napkin in half from right to left.

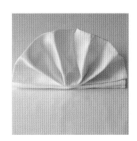

6 Let go of the pleats and they should fall down into a fan.

CANDLE NAPKIN

1 Start with a square flat napkin and fold the bottom right-hand corner point not quite up to the top left point of the napkin.

4 Roll the napkin up along the widest part of the fold.

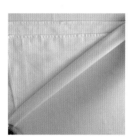

2 Fold the bottom edge over once.

5 Tuck the edge into the bottom fold.

3 Holding the fold carefully, turn the napkin over.

6 Your napkin should now stand up in the shape of a candle.

TIED FAN NAPKIN

1 Start with a flat square napkin and make a concertina pleat from the bottom edge.

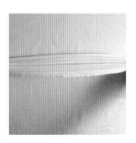

2 Continue to pleat the napkin right up to the top edge.

3 Fold the pleats in half.

4 Tie a ribbon to secure the pleated, halved napkin.

5 Lay the napkin on its edge with the bow facing you.

6 Fan the top of the napkin out.

OYSTERS FINDLAY, PAGE 36

STARTERS

★

HONEY ROASTED SALMON WITH MOUSSELINE SAUCE

Serves 4

Honey brings a gentle, not overpowering, sweetness to this dish. You can prepare the salmon parcels earlier in the day and refrigerate. This would also be a perfect light meal for lunch, served with a small side salad and fresh crusty bread.

SALMON:
Tin foil, 4 squares 10 x 10 inch (25 x 25 cm)
Olive oil for greasing foil
4 salmon portions, 5 oz (140 g) each
2 tbsp (30 mL) liquid honey

MOUSSELINE SAUCE:
½ cup (125 mL) heavy cream (35% m.f.)
½ cup (125 mL) butter
3 egg yolks
2 tbsp (30 mL) lemon juice
¼ tsp (1 mL) salt
Chives for garnish

For the salmon:

Preheat oven to 350°F (180°C).

Lightly brush foil with olive oil to ensure fish does not stick while baking. Rinse salmon under cold running water, pat dry and place each portion onto foil.

Brush a coating of honey over each salmon piece. Fold foil to form a loose package enclosing salmon. Arrange packages on a baking sheet and bake for 12 to 15 minutes.

Make Mousseline sauce while salmon is baking.

For the Mousseline sauce:

In a mixer, beat cream until stiff peaks form; reserve.

In a microwave oven or on a stovetop, heat butter until completely melted and very hot.

In a blender, add egg yolks, lemon juice and salt; process a few seconds to combine. With blender on high speed, slowly pour hot butter in a steady stream through the removable opening in the blender cover. The sauce will have thickened in the time it takes to add the hot butter, about 30 seconds.

Remove sauce to a warm bowl, fold in reserved whipped cream and keep warm.

Spoon a small amount of sauce on serving dishes; position salmon portions in the centre and top with additional sauce. Garnish with fresh chives.

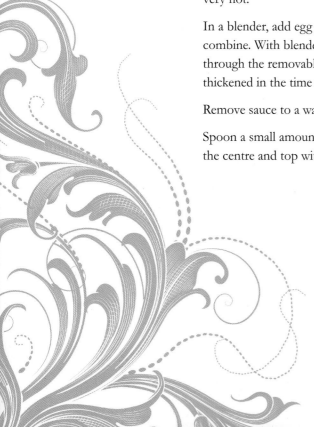

CABBAGE AU GRATIN

Serves 4

This dish may take a little more time to prepare than basic boiled cabbage, but once ready, it just needs a short time in the oven.

CABBAGE:

1 ½ lb (675 g) cabbage, shredded
1 ½ cups (375 mL) Béchamel sauce (recipe follows)
4 tbsp (60 mL) heavy cream (35% m.f.)
1 tsp (5 mL) mustard powder
Salt and pepper
3 oz (80 g) cheddar cheese, grated, divided
½ cup (125 mL) fresh bread crumbs
3 tbsp (45 mL) butter, plus extra for greasing

Preheat oven to 375°F (190°C).

Bring a saucepan of lightly salted water to boil and cook cabbage for 4 minutes; drain well.

Gently heat the Béchamel sauce in a large pan and add cream, mustard powder and salt and pepper. Stir to combine.

Stir in the well-drained cabbage and gently heat through.

Remove saucepan from heat and stir in 2 ounces (55 g) of cheese.

Grease a 2 quart (1.8 L) ovenproof dish and fill with cabbage mixture.

In a bowl, mix together bread crumbs and remaining cheese. Sprinkle crumb mixture over cabbage, dot with butter and bake until top is golden and crispy, about 20 minutes.

BÉCHAMEL SAUCE

Makes 1 ½ cups (375 mL)

1 ¼ cups (310 mL) homogenized milk
1 medium onion, halved
2 bay leaves
6 peppercorns
2 tbsp (30 mL) butter
2 tbsp (30 mL) all-purpose flour
Pinch of nutmeg

In a saucepan, bring milk, onion, bay leaves and peppercorns to just under a boil. Remove from heat; leave to infuse and cool for 1 hour.

Strain milk, discarding the onion and seasoning; set aside.

In a saucepan, melt butter over medium heat, whisk in flour and nutmeg and cook, stirring constantly to make a roux, about 1 minute.

Gradually whisk milk into the roux. Continue to cook sauce, stirring constantly until thickened.

PEA SOUP

★ ★ ★

Serves 4

This delicate soup has a delicious flavour and striking bright green colour that presents very well as a first course.

3 tbsp (45 mL) butter
4 shallots, finely sliced
1 clove garlic, minced
4 cups (1 L) chicken stock
4 ½ cups (1.125 L) fresh or frozen shelled peas
⅓ cup (75 mL) heavy cream (35% m.f.)
Salt and pepper
1 cup (250 mL) crème fraiche (recipe follows)

In a heavy-based saucepan, melt butter over medium-low heat. Add shallots and garlic and sauté until softened, about 5 minutes.

Add stock and peas and bring to a boil; reduce heat to low, cover and simmer until peas are tender, about 15 minutes.

In a blender, purée soup in batches until smooth. Strain soup through a sieve and return to saucepan.

Whisk cream into soup and adjust seasoning with salt and pepper. Bring to serving temperature.

Ladle in warmed soup bowls; garnish with a dollop of crème fraiche.

CRÈME FRAICHE

Makes 1 cup (250 mL)

Do not use heavy cream that is ultra-pasteurized or UHT (ultra high temperature) pasteurized.

1 cup (250 mL) heavy cream (35% m.f.)
2 tbsp (30 mL) buttermilk

In a small glass bowl, combine cream and buttermilk. Cover and let stand at room temperature for 8 to 24 hours or until thickened. Stir and refrigerate for up to 10 days.

DUCK LIVER PÂTÉ WITH TOAST POINTS

★ ★ ★

Serves 4

Serve the pâté with warm toast points or crackers.

PÂTÉ:
½ lb (225 g) duck livers
Milk
6 tbsp (90 mL) butter, softened, divided
2 tsp (10 mL) brandy
1 tsp (5 mL) chopped fresh rosemary
Salt and pepper
3 tbsp (45 mL) melted butter

TOAST POINTS:
1 loaf white bread, crust removed
¼ cup (60 mL) olive oil
1 tsp (5 mL) sea salt
Rosemary sprigs for garnish

For the pâté:

De-vein and trim livers and place in a bowl with enough milk to completely cover. Refrigerate and soak overnight if possible. When ready to cook, remove livers from milk and pat dry with paper towels.

Heat 3 tablespoons (45 mL) of softened butter in a skillet over medium heat; add livers and cook gently for 3 to 4 minutes. The livers should be cooked on the outside but a little pink inside. Remove from skillet and reserve.

Over medium heat, deglaze skillet with brandy and rosemary, scraping up the residue of the livers.

In a food processor, add livers and pulse until smooth. Add heated brandy mixture, remaining 3 tablespoons (45 mL) of softened butter and process until smooth. Season with salt and pepper to taste.

Spoon pâté into individual ramekins and pour melted butter over the tops to seal. Cover ramekins and refrigerate.

For the toast points:

Preheat oven to 350°F (180°C).

Slice bread to make 10 thin slices ¼ inch (5 mm) thick. Cut slices into triangles and lightly brush both sides with olive oil. Place bread on a baking sheet and lightly sprinkle with sea salt. Bake, turning once, until golden and curled up at the edges, about 8 to 10 minutes.

To serve, place each pâté ramekin on a dining plate, arrange toasted triangles around the sides and garnish with a sprig of fresh rosemary.

CREAM OF BARLEY SOUP

★ ★ ★

Serves 4

In the original Titanic *menu this soup would have been laced with double cream just before serving. Lighter crème fraiche has been substituted. Use beef stock for a richer, hearty flavour or chicken stock for a more delicate taste.*

1 tbsp (15 mL) butter
⅔ cup (150 mL) diced carrot
⅔ cup (150 mL) diced celery
⅔ cup (150 mL) diced onion
1 clove garlic, minced
5 cups (1.25 L) beef or chicken stock
⅔ cup (150 mL) pearl barley, rinsed
2 bay leaves
Salt and pepper
4 tbsp (60 mL) crème fraiche
   (see page 28)
2 slices crisp bacon, crumbled

In a stockpot, heat butter over low heat and add carrot, celery, onion and garlic. Cover pot and sweat vegetables, until softened, about 10 to 15 minutes.
Add stock, pearl barley and bay leaves, bring to a boil and then reduce heat to simmer. Skim the top as necessary and gently cook the soup for 45 minutes.

Cool soup slightly and discard bay leaves.

In a blender, purée in batches and return to stockpot. Return to serving temperature and adjust seasoning with salt and pepper.

Serve in warmed soup bowls with a dollop of crème fraiche and a sprinkling of crumbled crisp bacon.

COLD ASPARAGUS VINAIGRETTE

Serves 4

This dish was served as a starter course in first class at dinnertime. The asparagus can easily be prepared beforehand and refrigerated until you are ready to plate the dish.

1 lb (450 g) fresh asparagus
1 tsp (5 mL) minced shallot
½ tsp (2 mL) Dijon mustard
1 tsp (5 mL) lemon zest
1 tbsp (15 mL) lemon juice
3 tbsp (45 mL) olive oil
Dash of salt and pepper

Break ends off asparagus and wash stalks well. Bring a skillet of water to a boil; add asparagus and cook until al dente, about 4 to 6 minutes. Cooking time will depend on the thickness of the asparagus.

Drain asparagus and plunge into an ice bath to stop cooking process. Pat dry with paper towels and refrigerate, covered with plastic wrap.

Make vinaigrette. In a jar, combine the remaining ingredients. Cover and shake well until emulsified. Refrigerate.

Twenty minutes before serving, arrange asparagus on a serving platter and drizzle with vinaigrette.

RICE SOUP

Serves 4

This easy-to-prepare soup contains ingredients common to the Titanic *era. Serve as prepared with rustic bread and cheese for a hearty lunch or topped with croutons for a light starter.*

2 tbsp (30 mL) butter
¾ cup (175 mL) medium-diced carrot
¾ cup (175 mL) chopped onion
¾ cup (175 mL) medium-diced parsnip
2 cloves garlic, minced
3 cups (750 mL) chicken stock
2 tbsp (30 mL) light soy sauce
½ cup (125 mL) long grain rice
1 ¼ cups (310 mL) water
Salt and pepper

Heat butter in a large, heavy-based saucepan over medium-low heat. Add carrot, onion, parsnip and garlic and sauté for 10 minutes, stirring frequently.

Add chicken stock and soy sauce. Bring to a boil, reduce heat and simmer until the vegetables are tender, about 15 minutes.

While vegetables are simmering, cook rice. In a saucepan bring water to a boil, add rice; reduce heat to low and simmer until water is absorbed, about 15 minutes.

Add cooked rice to soup, adjust seasoning and bring back to serving temperature.

OYSTERS FINDLAY

★ ★ ★

Serves 4

Not only does this starter look impressive but it tastes good too.

Always take care when preparing oysters. Clean oyster shells with a stiff kitchen brush. Protect your hand with a folded towel and open the shells by levering the point of a strong, dull knife between the two halves. When the oyster is open, cut the muscle; remove and discard the flat top shell. Slide a knife under the oyster to loosen it and leave the oyster on the bottom shell.

12 oysters, cleaned and opened, flat shell discarded

4 tbsp (60 mL) softened butter

1 tbsp (15 mL) chopped fresh parsley

2 tsp (10 mL) Dijon mustard

1 clove garlic, minced

1 cup (250 mL) soft bread crumbs

½ cup (125 mL) finely grated Parmesan cheese

Zest of 1 lemon

Edible greens for serving

2 lemons, quartered, for garnish

Preheat oven to 400°F (200°C).

Place the oysters on bottom shells in a steamer and steam for 3 minutes. Reserve and cool.

In a small bowl combine butter, parsley, mustard and garlic. Portion equal amounts on each deep shell half.

Place 1 oyster on top of butter mixture in each shell.

In a medium bowl, combine bread crumbs, cheese and lemon zest.

Sprinkle crumb mixture evenly over each oyster. Place oysters on a baking sheet and bake for 15 minutes, until crumbs are golden.

To serve, arrange edible greens on 4 individual plates, set oysters on greens and garnish with lemon quarters.

ROAST LAMB WITH STRAWBERRY MINT GRAVY, PAGE 40

MAIN COURSES

★

ROAST LAMB WITH STRAWBERRY MINT GRAVY

Serves 6

We suggest serving this elegant dish with Parsnip and Potato Mash (see page 86) and a green vegetable. Any leftover meat and gravy is delicious warmed and served with steamed vegetables.

3 tbsp (45 mL) vegetable oil
1 leg of lamb, 4 lb (1.85 kg)
4 tbsp (60 mL) finely chopped fresh mint
2 tbsp (30 mL) boiling water
2 tsp (10 mL) granulated sugar
2 tbsp (30 mL) white wine vinegar
16 strawberries, hulled
1 chicken stock cube, crumbed
3 tbsp (45 mL) all-purpose flour
4 cups (1 L) vegetable stock

Preheat oven to 325°F (170°C).

Heat oil in a heavy skillet over moderately high heat and sear the lamb on all sides, about 4 minutes total.

Place lamb in a roasting pan, together with the pan oil and brown bits from the frying pan. Cover with foil and roast 1 hour. Remove foil and roast until meat reaches 145°F (60°C) for rare or 160°F (70°C) for medium, approximately 30 to 40 minutes longer.

While meat is cooking, place mint, boiling water, sugar and vinegar into a small bowl. Stir and set aside to infuse.

Hull strawberries and mash. Push the strawberries through a sieve and add the strawberry pulp to the mint mixture.

When meat is cooked, remove from oven; cover loosely with foil and let sit for 10 minutes.

Skim most of the fat from the pan and discard. Place pan with remaining juices on a burner over low heat. Add stock cube and sprinkle in flour, stirring and scraping up the lamb residue from the bottom of the pan.

Gradually add vegetable stock, 1 cup (250 mL) at a time, stirring thoroughly after each addition until gravy has thickened.

Stir mint mixture into gravy. Add additional boiling water if a thinner gravy is preferred. Strain gravy into a saucepan, cover and keep hot.

Slice lamb and serve with gravy.

FILET MIGNON LILI

Serves 4

This easy-to-prepare dish is sure to please the most discriminating palate. Serve remaining sauce in a gravy boat at the table.

POTATOES:
6 large potatoes, peeled, thinly sliced
Cold water
2 tsp (10 mL) lemon juice
½ cup (125 mL) melted butter, plus extra for greasing
Salt and pepper

MADEIRA SAUCE:
3 tbsp (45 mL) all-purpose flour
1 tbsp (15 mL) butter
1 cup (250 mL beef stock
1 cup (250 mL) Madeira wine

STEAK:
Salt and pepper
4 beef tenderloin filets, 6 oz (170 g) each
4 thin slices bacon, centre cut
2 tbsp (30 mL) olive oil
1 tbsp (15 mL) butter

For the potatoes:
Preheat oven to 400°F (200°C).

Grease a 2-quart (1.8 L) ovenproof dish.

Peel potatoes and place in a large bowl, cover with cold water and stir in lemon juice. When ready to prepare potato dish, drain potatoes and pat dry.

Arrange one layer of potato, overlapping, in bottom of baking dish; brush with melted butter and season with salt and pepper. Repeat this process in layers for the remaining potato slices. Bake, uncovered, until lightly golden and tender, approximately 35 to 40 minutes.

For the Madeira sauce:
Combine flour and butter with your fingers and roll into small balls; reserve.

In a saucepan, combine stock and wine; bring to a simmer over medium heat and whisk in butter balls, one at a time, until the sauce is thick and smooth. Reduce heat and simmer, stirring, for 2 minutes. Keep warm until needed.

For the steak:
Season steak with salt and pepper. Wrap steaks with bacon and secure with a toothpick. Heat oil and butter in a heavy-based skillet.

Add fillets to skillet and cook, turning once, until brown. Allow about 3 minutes per side for rare, and 4 minutes per side for medium. Remember, cooking times vary depending upon the thickness of the steak. Remove toothpicks.

To serve, place a wedge of the potato on a warm plate and arrange steak on top. Serve a little sauce with the steaks and place remaining sauce in a gravy boat to serve at the table.

ROAST TURKEY WITH GRAVY AND CRANBERRY SAUCE

★ ★ ★

Serves 6

Roast turkey accompanied by cranberry sauce need not be saved for a special occasion.

TURKEY:
8 lb (3.62 kg) butter-basted turkey
1 lemon, halved
1 onion, peeled and halved
Small bunch of herbs (sage, parsley, thyme, etc.)
1 tbsp (15 mL) vegetable oil

CRANBERRY SAUCE:
1 cup (250 mL) water
1 cup (250 mL) granulated sugar
12 oz (375 g) fresh cranberries
2 tbsp (30 mL) butter
3 tbsp (45 mL) port

GRAVY:
1 chicken stock cube, crumbled
3 tbsp (45 mL) all-purpose flour
4 cups (1 L) vegetable stock

For the turkey:

Preheat oven to 325°F (160°C).

Remove giblets and neck from turkey.

Wash turkey in cold water and pat dry. Place lemon, onion and herbs inside turkey cavity.

Rub turkey with vegetable oil and roast in a heavy roasting pan, allowing 20 minutes per pound (500 g) until internal temperature of the thickest part of turkey thigh registers 175°F (80°C).

During baking, baste occasionally with drippings. If turkey is becoming too brown, tent with foil. When done, remove turkey to a platter, tent with foil and let sit for 20 to 30 minutes.

For the cranberry sauce:

In a saucepan, combine water and sugar over low heat and stir until sugar has dissolved.

Add cranberries and cook over high heat, stirring occasionally, until skins begin to pop, about 6 to 8 minutes.

Reduce heat and simmer, uncovered, stirring occasionally, 15 to 20 minutes. The berries should be softened and the liquid reduced.

Remove saucepan from heat and stir in butter and port.

Refrigerate until needed.

For the gravy:

Remove onion, lemon and herbs from turkey cavity; reserve.

Skim fat from juices in roasting pan; discard. Place remaining juices in pan on stovetop over medium heat.

Add stock cube and flour to the pan juices and whisk until incorporated, scraping up any bits from the bottom of the pan. Add reserved onion mixture.

Gradually add stock, 1 cup (250 mL) at a time, stirring after each addition, until gravy thickens. Add boiling water if a thinner gravy is preferred.

Before serving, strain gravy into a saucepan. Simmer gently 3 minutes and serve.

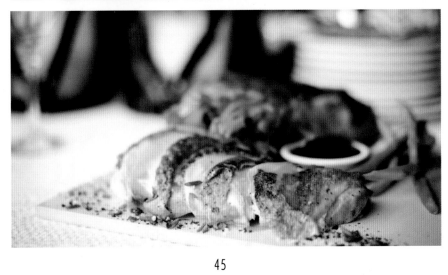

CHICKEN LYONNAISE

★ ★ ★

Serves 4

Simple to prepare, the ingredients in this dish are reduced to a delicious sauce. We suggest serving the chicken with a savoury rice pilaf.

¼ cup (60 mL) all-purpose flour
½ tsp (2 mL) salt
¼ tsp (1 mL) pepper
4 chicken breasts, 6 oz (170 g) each
2 tbsp (30 mL) butter
1 tbsp (15 mL) olive oil
1 medium onion, sliced
1 tbsp (15 mL) tomato paste
1 clove garlic, minced
½ cup (125 mL) white wine
½ cup (125 mL) cognac
2 tbsp (30 mL) granulated sugar
¼ cup (60 mL) chicken stock

Place flour, salt and pepper in a plastic bag; add chicken and toss to coat.

In a large skillet over medium-high heat, combine butter and oil. Add chicken and brown on all sides; remove from skillet and reserve.

Add onion to skillet and cook until soft, about 5 minutes. Stir tomato paste, garlic, wine, cognac, sugar and stock into skillet until combined. Add chicken to skillet and spoon sauce over top. Cook gently, uncovered, on medium-low heat until cooked, about 15 to 20 minutes.

Adjust seasoning to taste. Serve chicken topped with sauce.

IRISH STEW WITH DUMPLINGS

Serves 4

How fitting to serve a dish from "the old country" to passengers making the journey to "the new world" on the Titanic!

STEW:
3 tbsp (45 mL) butter
1 ½ lb (680 g) lamb, cubed
1 large onion, sliced
4 potatoes, peeled and quartered
2 carrots, sliced
2 cups (500 mL) shredded cabbage
2 cups (500 mL) chicken stock
1 cup (250 mL) stout beer
Salt and pepper

DUMPLINGS:
1 cup (250 mL) self-rising flour
½ tsp (2 mL) salt
2 tbsp (30 mL) shortening
½ cup (125 mL) homogenized milk

For the stew:

Melt butter in a large, heavy-based saucepan and sear meat over medium-high heat, about 5 minutes, until browned. Remove meat from pan and reserve.

Reduce heat to medium-low, add onion and cook until softened, about 5 minutes.

Return meat to pan, together with potatoes, carrots, cabbage, stock and stout.

Bring to a boil, season with salt and pepper, reduce heat to simmer and cook, covered, for 15 minutes.

For the dumplings:

In a medium bowl, mix together flour and salt. Using a pastry blender, cut in shortening. Add enough milk to make a sticky dough.

Uncover pot and drop spoonfuls of dumpling dough on top of stew. Cover and simmer an additional 30 minutes. Serve in warmed bowls.

ZUCCHINI FARCIE

★ ★ ★

Serves 4

Zucchini, somewhat similar to its cousin vegetable marrow, is rather bland in flavour. Stuffing zucchini with a savoury filling elevates the vegetable to new heights.

4 tbsp (60 mL) olive oil, plus a little extra for brushing
2 medium onions, finely chopped
1 lb (450 g) lean ground beef
1 tbsp (15 mL) chopped parsley
1 tbsp (15 mL) tomato paste
½ tsp (2 mL) paprika
¾ cup (175 mL) beef stock
Salt and pepper
2 medium zucchinis, about 12 in (30.5 cm) in length
½ cup (125 mL) grated cheddar cheese

Preheat oven to 350°F (180°C).

Heat oil in a large skillet. Add onion and sauté 5 minutes over medium heat.

Add beef and cook, stirring occasionally, until no longer pink, approximately 5 minutes.

Add parsley, tomato paste, paprika and stock and stir well to combine.

Simmer until thickened, approximately 15 minutes. When thick, remove from heat, season with salt and pepper and reserve.

Trim and halve the zucchinis into 4 portions. Scoop out the seeds and cut a thin slice from the bottoms so they will sit level.

Brush the insides of zucchinis with oil. Fill the cavities with beef mixture, covering the flesh completely.

Top with cheese, place on a baking sheet and bake for 30 minutes or until zucchini is tender.

HADDOCK WITH SHARP SAUCE

★ ★ ★

Serves 4

Sweet mild haddock has been a food staple for years. The sauce, which is prepared in advance, brings out the wow factor of this dish.

SHARP SAUCE:

- 1 can diced tomatoes, 14 oz (400 mL)
- 1 small onion, coarsely chopped
- 1 stalk celery, coarsely chopped
- ½ cup (125 mL) chopped green pepper
- Several drops of Tabasco sauce
- ½ tsp (2 mL) pepper
- 1 ½ tbsp (22 mL) minced fresh parsley

HADDOCK:

- 4 haddock fillets, 6 oz (170 g) each
- ¼ cup (60 mL) all-purpose flour
- ¼ tsp (1 mL) salt
- ¼ tsp (1 mL) pepper
- 1 tbsp (15 mL) chopped fresh parsley
- ½ tsp (2 mL) paprika
- 1 tbsp (15 mL) vegetable oil
- 2 tbsp (30 mL) butter

For the sharp sauce:

Combine all ingredients in a heavy-based saucepan; cook over low heat for 1 hour or until thickened.

Break up tomatoes as the sauce simmers and stir often as it will burn easily. Reserve and keep warm.

For the haddock:

Remove bones from haddock portions.

In a medium bowl, combine flour, salt, pepper, parsley and paprika; mix well. Dredge fish in flour mixture.

In a skillet, heat oil and butter over medium-high heat; add fillets and sauté, turning once, allowing 8 to 10 minutes per inch of thickness. Fish is cooked when it flakes easily and is opaque.

Portion fillets on plates and top with sharp sauce.

CURRIED CHICKEN

★ ★ ★

Serves 4

2 tbsp (30 mL) vegetable oil

4 boneless, skinless, chicken breasts, about 6 oz (170 g) each

1 medium onion, chopped

1 in (2.5 cm) fresh ginger, peeled and minced

2 cloves garlic, minced

2 tbsp (30 mL) mild curry powder

½ cup (125 mL) plain yogurt

1 tbsp (15 mL) tomato paste

1 ½ cups (375 mL) coconut milk

¾ cup (175 mL) chicken stock

1 ripe mango, peeled and cut into bite-sized chunks

In a large, heavy-based saucepan, heat oil over medium-high heat; add chicken and brown on both sides, approximately 4 minutes. Remove chicken and reserve.

Add onion to saucepan, reduce heat to medium and cook until onion is softened, about 5 minutes. Stir in ginger, garlic and curry powder and cook 1 minute longer.

Add yogurt, tomato paste, coconut milk and stock to the saucepan; stir to combine.

Add chicken and simmer until chicken is cooked and sauce is reduced, about 30 to 40 minutes. Add mango to curry a few minutes before removing from heat.

Serve with rice, accompanied by banana slices, raisins and chutney.

SIRLOIN STEAK WITH CREAMY MUSTARD SAUCE

Serves 4

Many people still opt for steak when dining out, so this dish will continue to please for many years to come! Served with a delicious mustard sauce and accompanied by mushrooms, tomatoes and Pommes Parmentier (see page 89), it can't fail to impress.

MUSTARD SAUCE:

3 tbsp (45 mL) butter, cubed
3 tbsp (45 mL) all-purpose flour
2 tbsp (30 mL) dry mustard
1 cup (250 mL) homogenized milk
3 tbsp (45 mL) heavy cream
   (35% m.f.)

STEAKS:

4 sirloin steaks, 6 oz (170 g) each
Salt and pepper

For the sauce:

In a saucepan over medium heat, melt butter; stir in flour and mustard powder to form a roux. Add milk and cook, whisking constantly, until thick and creamy. Remove from heat and stir in cream. Keep warm until needed.

For the steak:

Season steak with salt and pepper.

Grill steaks on high heat until cooked to desired doneness. Serve with sauce.

ROAST DUCK WITH APPLE SAUCE

★ ★ ★

Serves 4

Duck can be very fatty, so you will need to roast it on a rack in an oven roaster. This entree pairs well with roasted vegetables.

APPLE SAUCE:
4 large cooking apples, such as Cortland, Spartan or Granny Smith
⅓ cup (100 mL) water
1 tbsp (15 mL) granulated sugar
1 tsp (5 mL) ground cinnamon

ROAST DUCK:
1 duckling, approximately 5 to 6 lbs (2.5 to 3 kg)
Salt and pepper

For the apple sauce:
Peel, core and dice apples.

In a saucepan, combine apples, water, sugar and cinnamon and cook over medium heat until apples are soft but not completely broken down, about 5 to 7 minutes.

Pour sauce into a bowl, cover and refrigerate until needed.

For the roast duck:
Preheat oven to 425°F (220°C).

Place duck on a cutting board and remove all visible fat from neck and cavity. Wash duck inside and out, pat dry, then prick skin all over with a fork. This will allow fat to escape during roasting. Rub salt and pepper into the skin.

Place seasoned duck on a rack in a roaster and roast breast side up for 45 minutes. Turn duck breast side down and roast another 45 minutes. Turn breast side up and continue to bake until a thermometer inserted in the thickest part of the thigh registers 175°F (80°C), approximately 45 minutes longer.

Remove duck from oven, drain juices from cavity and let rest 15 minutes. Carve and serve with apple sauce.

JACKET POTATOES WITH CHEESE

★ ★ ★

Serves 4

2 large baking potatoes
2 to 3 tbsp (30 to 45 mL) sour cream
6 tbsp (90 mL) cheddar cheese,
grated, divided
1 tbsp (15 mL) minced fresh parsley
Salt and pepper

Preheat oven to 400°F (200°C).

Scrub potatoes, pat dry and pierce several times with a sharp knife. Place potatoes on a baking sheet and bake 1 hour or until tender. Remove from oven and set aside until cool enough to handle.

Cut each potato in half lengthwise; scoop flesh carefully from potato halves and reserve in a bowl.

Mash potatoes until smooth. Stir in sour cream, half of the cheese and parsley. Season with salt and pepper.

Spoon potato mixture back into potato skins, top with remaining cheese and bake an additional 10 to 15 minutes until piping hot and cheese has melted.

DESSERTS

★

APPLE MERINGUE PIE

★ ★ ★

Serves 6

This pie is a pleasant alternative to the sharper lemon version that is more commonly prepared. It is best eaten on the same day as it is baked.

6 cooking apples, about 2 lb (1.5 kg)
½ cup (125 mL) granulated sugar
¼ cup (60 mL) water
1 tsp (5 mL) ground cinnamon
Pinch of nutmeg
1 prebaked pie shell
3 egg whites, at room temperature,
¼ tsp (1 mL) cream of tartar
Fresh fruit garnish (optional)

Preheat oven to 400°F (200°C).

Peel, core and chop apples. In a large saucepan over medium-low heat, combine apples, half the sugar and water.

Bring to a simmer, reduce heat to low and cook slowly, stirring often, until apples are soft, about 15 to 20 minutes.

Place apple mixture in a fine-mesh sieve and drain, about 10 minutes.

Remove apple mixture to a large bowl and stir in cinnamon and nutmeg; reserve.

Place apple mixture into baked pie shell.

Make meringue. In a mixer beat egg whites until soft peaks form, about 2 minutes. Slowly beat in cream of tartar and remaining sugar and beat until meringue is glossy and forms stiff peaks when beaters are lifted.

Spoon meringue over apple mixture, completely covering apples and making sure it goes to the crust edge.

Bake for 8 to 12 minutes or until meringue is golden. Remove from oven and cool.

For presentation, garnish with fresh fruit if desired.

FRESH FRUIT WITH SWEET CREAMED CHEESE

Serves 4

Strawberry coulis drizzled over the fruit would finish this dish off perfectly. To make a coulis: hull 2 cups (500 mL) strawberries; place them in a food processor together with 1 tbsp (15 mL) icing sugar. Process until smooth and then pass through a sieve. Refrigerate until ready to use.

1 cup (250 mL) mascarpone cheese
1 tsp (5 mL) orange zest, minced
2 tbsp (30 mL) honey
2 tbsp (30 mL) heavy cream
   (35% m.f.)
4 kiwi fruits, peeled and sliced
12 strawberries, hulled and cut
   vertically in heart shapes
12 grapes, halved
1 banana, sliced
Additional fresh fruit for garnish

In a mixer on low speed, mix cheese, zest and honey until smooth. Add cream a little at a time until you get an easily spreadable consistency, adding more cream if necessary.

Prepare fruit and arrange slices on centre of serving plates. Use a ring mold if you prefer a neater look.

Alternate fruit and cheese in layers, finishing with the cheese and a crown of fruit.

CHEESE TRAY

★ ★ ★

Serves 4. Choose 3 or 4 different cheeses and allow 1 to 2 oz (25 to 55 g) of each cheese per person.

The Titanic *menu lists cheeses to be offered at the end of luncheons in first and second class and after dinner in second class. For those travelling in third class, cheese in the singular was offered with Cabin Biscuits (see page 73).*

Cheshire
Stilton
Gorgonzola
Roquefort
Camembert
Edam
St. Ivel
Cheddar

On a cheese tray, arrange 3 or 4 cheeses from the suggested list. Cheeses should be served at room temperature.

Garnish your tray with a fresh grapes, nuts and dried fruits and accompany with a selection of fine biscuits.

BAKED APPLES

Serves 4

Make sure you use baking apples of the same size. Golden Delicious, Granny Smith, Cortland and McIntosh apples all work well in this recipe, but feel free to use an apple that appeals to your taste. Remember that a firmer apple variety may require a slightly longer cooking time.

4 baking apples
½ cup (125 mL) chopped mixed
   dried fruit (apricots, figs, prunes,
   raisins, etc.)
¼ cup (60 mL) brown sugar, plus
   a little extra to sprinkle over the
   apples before baking
½ tsp (2 mL) ground cinnamon
2 tbsp (30 mL) butter

Preheat oven to 375°F (190°C).

Core apples just short of the bottom so that the base is still intact. With a knife, level bottoms so that apples will remain upright during baking. With a paring knife, peel a ½-inch (1 cm) circular strip at the top and make a shallow cut horizontally around the centre of each apple. Place apples in a shallow baking dish.

In a small bowl, mix together dried fruit, sugar and cinnamon. Portion fruit mixture into apple cavities; dab with butter and sprinkle with extra sugar.

Pour a little water around the base of the apples; bake for 40 minutes or until apples are cooked. Test for doneness with a toothpick; if it goes in smoothly the apple is cooked.

Serve with crème fraiche (see page 28) or custard (see page 93).

CHOCOLATE GANACHE ECLAIRS

Serves 6, makes 12 eclairs

Filling these eclairs with chocolate ganache produces an extremely decadent and luxurious dessert. They may also be filled with sweetened whipped cream with equal success.

CHOCOLATE GANACHE:
**6 oz (170 g) good quality dark
chocolate**
**1 cup (250 mL) heavy cream
(35% m.f.)**
Pinch of salt

ECLAIRS:
**1 cup (250 mL) all-purpose flour,
sifted**
Pinch of salt
1 tbsp (15 mL) granulated sugar
1 cup (250 mL) water
½ cup (125 mL) butter
4 eggs at room temperature
**3 oz (80 g) good quality dark
chocolate**

For the ganache:

Finely chop chocolate and place in a heatproof bowl.

In a saucepan over medium-high heat, bring cream to a boil; remove from heat and pour over chocolate.

Let cream and chocolate rest for 1 minute. With a whisk, stir the mixture until the chocolate melts and then whisk briskly until the ganache is smooth and satiny. Whisk in the salt and continue beating until the ganache cools, and thickens enough to become spreadable. Be careful not to over whip as the ganache will become granular.

Reserve in refrigerator.

For the eclairs:

Preheat oven to 400°F (200°C).

In a small bowl, combine flour, salt and sugar.

In a saucepan over medium heat, bring water and butter to a boil. Add flour mixture, all at once, and beat vigorously with a wooden spoon until batter begins to dry and leaves the side of the pan, about 2 to 3 minutes. Do not overcook.

Remove pan from heat and let rest 2 minutes. Add eggs, one at a time, beating vigorously after each addition. Continue beating until all eggs are incorporated. The batter is ready if it stands erect when you scoop a small amount onto a spoon.

Drop batter from a spoon, 2 inches (5 cm) apart onto a baking sheet lined with parchment paper. Bake for 10 minutes; reduce heat to 350°F (180°C) and bake 25 minutes longer or until eclairs are lightly golden and firm to the touch. Cool on a wire rack.

When cool, cut eclairs horizontally with a sharp knife. Remove any dough that is not totally dry inside the cavity. Fill a piping bag with the ganache and pipe into cavities. Alternatively, using a teaspoon, fill cavities with the ganache.

Melt chocolate in a bowl over a saucepan of hot water, making sure that the water does not touch the bowl.

With a spoon, spread or zigzag a layer of melted chocolate over each eclair. Leave to set at room temperature.

RICE PUDDING

Serves 4 to 6

Medium-grain rice works well in this pudding recipe; it tends to be more moist than long-grain rice and not as starchy as short-grain. If it is not available, feel free to substitute regular long-grain rice. This is comfort food at its best, equally loved by young and old.

1 tbsp (15 mL) butter, plus extra for greasing
2 cups (500 mL) homogenized milk
½ cup (125 mL) granulated sugar
2 eggs
1 tsp (5 mL) vanilla extract
Pinch of salt
2 cups (500 mL) cooked rice
¼ tsp (1 mL) ground nutmeg

Preheat oven to 325°F (160°C).

Grease a 2-quart (1.8 L) ovenproof dish with butter.

In a large bowl, beat together milk, sugar, eggs, vanilla and salt until well combined. Add the cooked rice and stir to combine.

Pour the mixture into the greased ovenproof dish and dot with butter.

Bake for 15 minutes, then stir and sprinkle with nutmeg. Return to oven and bake another 20 minutes.

WALDORF PUDDING

Serves 4

The term "pudding" in the United Kingdom is often just another name for dessert. During the Edwardian era, puddings were a traditional ending to meals.

No one has been able to find the exact recipe for the Waldorf pudding listed on the Titanic *menu, but it is generally agreed that it probably included apples, raisins and some type of sweet, cake-like batter.*

4 large cooking apples, cored, peeled and thinly sliced
½ cup (125 mL) raisins
1 tsp (5 mL) ground cinnamon
Pinch of ground nutmeg
½ cup (125 mL) brown sugar
1 cup (250 mL) all-purpose flour
½ cup (125 mL) granulated sugar
½ cup (125 mL) butter

Preheat oven to 350°F (180°C).

Grease a 2-quart (1.8 L) baking dish with butter.

In a large bowl, combine apples, raisins, cinnamon, nutmeg and brown sugar; toss to coat. Add mixture to the baking dish.

In a medium bowl, mix together flour and granulated sugar. With a pastry blender, cut butter into flour mixture until it resembles coarse crumbs.

Top apples with the flour mixture, making sure it completely covers the apples.

Bake for 35 to 40 minutes or until apples are cooked and top is golden.

Serve with hot custard sauce (see page 89).

OLD-FASHIONED BREAD PUDDING, PAGE 74

AFTERNOON TEA

★

FRUIT SCONES

★ ★ ★

Makes 8 scones

Scones are very easy to make! To ensure a light mixture, handle the dough as little as possible. You may put dried fruit directly into the dough, but if you prefer a softer fruit, cover fruit with orange juice and allow to plump for up to 4 hours. The height of a scone is a personal choice; since they rise slightly when baking, gauge the thickness to complement whatever filling you are using.

2 cups (500 mL) self-rising flour
¼ cup (60 mL) granulated sugar
½ tsp (2 mL) salt
¼ cup (60 mL) butter, cubed, plus extra for greasing
¼ cup (60 mL) dried fruit
⅔ cup (150 mL) homogenized milk
1 egg, beaten

Preheat oven to 400°F (200°C).

In a bowl, combine flour, sugar and salt. With a pastry blender, cut butter into flour mixture until it resembles coarse crumbs.

Add fruit and mix to combine.

Slowly add milk to the mixture, stirring only until you get a manageable dough.

Pat dough out onto a floured surface to ½-inch (4 cm) thickness.

Cut scones with a round cutter and place on a greased baking sheet. Brush with beaten egg.

Bake 15 minutes or until golden brown. Cool on a wire rack.

CABIN BISCUITS

Makes 20 biscuits

The addition of whole wheat flour to Cabin Biscuits gives them an interesting texture.

¾ cup (175 mL) whole wheat flour
1 cup (250 mL) all-purpose flour
1 tbsp (15 ml) baking powder
¼ tsp (1 mL) salt
⅔ cup (150 mL) granulated sugar,
   plus extra for sprinkling
¼ cup (60 mL) butter, plus extra for
   greasing
⅔ cup (150 mL) homogenized milk

Preheat oven to 400°F (200°C).

Sift flours, baking powder and salt into a large bowl. Stir in sugar.

Add butter to flour mixture and rub in until it resembles fine bread crumbs. Stir in enough milk to make a firm dough.

Roll dough out on a floured surface and cut into rounds.

Place the biscuits on a greased baking sheet and bake 15 minutes or until golden.

Remove from oven, sprinkle with sugar and cool on a wire rack.

OLD-FASHIONED BREAD PUDDING

Serves 4 to 6

Comfort food at its best! On the Titanic, *this recipe would call for "mixed spice," which is any combination of cinnamon, cloves, nutmeg and ginger. In this recipe, we used ground cinnamon and nutmeg.*

6 cups (1.5 L) day-old white bread, crusts removed, cubed
1 ¼ cups (310 mL) homogenized milk
¼ cup (60 mL) butter, melted and cooled, plus extra for greasing
⅓ cup (75 mL) granulated sugar, plus extra for sprinkling
1 tsp (5 mL) ground cinnamon
Pinch of ground nutmeg
2 eggs, beaten
¾ cup (175 mL) raisins

Preheat oven to 375°F (190°C).

Butter a 2-quart (1.8 L) ovenproof dish.

Place bread in a bowl and pour milk over top. Press bread down with a spatula and let stand 10 to 15 minutes to soften.

In a bowl, whisk together butter, sugar, cinnamon, nutmeg and eggs. Stir in raisins.

Stir egg mixture into bread mixture until combined.

Spoon into the greased dish and bake, in a water bath, 55 to 65 minutes or until the pudding is firm to the touch and a knife inserted in the centre comes out clean.

Serve warm, sprinkled with sugar.

FRUIT BUNS

Makes approximately 15 buns

Fruit buns are similar to the Easter treat Hot Cross Buns. Using instant quick-rise yeast will shorten the preparation time, but still yield beautiful buns.

4 cups (1 L) all-purpose flour
¾ cup (175 mL) butter, plus extra for greasing
⅔ cup (150 mL) superfine sugar
1 tsp (5 mL) ground cinnamon
1 ½ cups (375 mL) mixed dried fruit, chopped
¼ tsp (1 mL) salt
2 ¼ tsp (11 mL) instant quick-rise dried yeast
1 ¼ cups (300 mL) homogenized milk
1 egg, beaten

GLAZE:
¼ cup (60 mL) superfine sugar
¼ cup (60 mL) cold water

Preheat oven to 400°F (200°C).

Sift flour into a large bowl and cut in the butter with a pastry blender until it resembles coarse crumbs.

Stir in sugar, cinnamon, mixed fruit, salt and yeast.

In a saucepan, warm milk to 125°F (50°C). Whisk egg into milk and pour slowly into dry mixture, stirring until it resembles soft dough.

Turn dough out onto a floured board and knead 8 minutes, until dough is elastic in texture.

Divide dough and form into 15 balls; place on a greased baking sheet. Cover with oiled plastic wrap and leave to rise in a warm, draught-free place.

When the buns have doubled in size, about 1 hour, bake for 20 minutes, or until golden.

Cool buns on a wire rack.

For the glaze:
In a saucepan over medium heat, bring sugar and water to a boil. Reduce heat and simmer, stirring, until mixture resembles syrup.

Brush hot glaze over each bun and serve.

JAM TARTS

★ ★ ★

Makes 12 tarts

Jam tarts are simple to make and are a pretty addition to a dessert tray.

1 ½ cups (375 mL) self-rising flour,
   plus extra for dusting
2 tbsp (30 mL) icing sugar
Pinch of salt
½ cup (125 mL) butter, cubed
Ice water
1 egg white, lightly whisked
1 cup (250 mL) jam

Preheat oven to 375°F (190°C).

Sift flour, icing sugar and salt into a large bowl.

Cut butter into flour mixture using a pastry blender until the mixture resembles fine crumbs.

Add 1 tablespoon (15 mL) of ice water to the mixture and stir with a fork for about 30 seconds. Add water as necessary, 1 teaspoon (5 mL) at a time, until the dough begins to hold together. You should have a smooth, non-sticky pastry dough.

Wrap dough in plastic wrap and refrigerate for 30 minutes.

Roll dough out onto a floured surface to ¼-inch (5 mm) thickness.

Cut out enough circles to fill a tart pan.

Press pastry rounds gently into tart pan and prick with a fork.

Brush the inside of each tart with egg white. Bake until golden, about 6 to 8 minutes.

Remove pan from oven and half-fill each tart with jam. Return to oven and bake an additional 5 minutes.

Serve warm, garnished with a spoonful of whipped cream or custard.

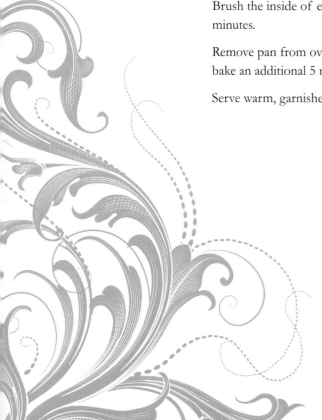

SHORTBREAD COOKIES

★ ★ ★

Makes 8 triangles

These traditional buttery cookies are hard to resist. A shortbread mold makes a beautiful presentation; however, the cookies can also be baked on a baking sheet.

1 ¼ cups (310 mL) all-purpose flour
⅓ cup (75 mL) cornstarch, plus extra
    for dusting mold
¼ cup (60 mL) superfine sugar, plus
    extra for sprinkling
½ cup (125 mL) butter, cubed

Preheat oven to 325°F (170°C).

Sift flour, cornstarch and sugar into a mixing bowl.

Using a pastry blender, cut butter into flour mixture. Turn out onto a floured board and knead until dough binds together and is smooth.

Lightly grease the inside of a shortbread mold and dust with a little cornstarch. Press the dough into the mold with your fingertips. Allow dough to set for 15 minutes. Put mold on a baking sheet.

If you are not using a mold, roll the dough into a circle, crimp the edges and place on a greased baking sheet.

Bake 25 to 35 minutes or until cookies are golden.

Remove shortbread from oven. With a sharp knife, mark the round into 8 triangles, being careful not to cut through. Sprinkle with sugar.

Cool on a wire rack. When completely cool, cut into triangles.

ACCOMPANIMENTS

LEMON CURD

Makes approximately 2 cups (500 mL)

You can change this recipe to make orange curd by using the zest of 2 oranges and lowering the sugar amount to 1 ⅓ cups (325 mL).

1 ⅔ cups (400 mL) superfine sugar
Zest from 3 lemons
½ cup (125 mL) butter, at room temperature
4 egg yolks
½ cup (125 mL) fresh lemon juice
Pinch of salt

In a food processor, combine sugar and lemon zest and pulse until zest is finely incorporated into the sugar, about 20 seconds.

In a mixer, cream butter and sugar mixture; add egg yolks, one at a time, beating after each addition. Add lemon juice and salt and combine well.

Pour mixture into a heavy-based 2-quart (1.8 L) saucepan and cook over low heat, stirring constantly until thickened, about 10 minutes.

When cooled, pour into clean, covered container and store refrigerated. Use within 10 days.

STRAWBERRY JAM

★ ★ ★

Makes about 8 cups (2 L)

4 cups (1 L) lightly crushed strawberries
¼ cup (60 mL) fresh lemon juice
7 cups (1.75 L) granulated sugar
1 pouch liquid fruit pectin

Wash and sterilize jars and prepare lids as per manufacturer's directions.

In a large saucepan, combine berries and lemon juice, being careful to fill pan no more than half full. Set over high heat and bring to a boil, stirring every few minutes. Add sugar and stir well, bringing back to a boil. Boil hard for 1 minute.

Remove from heat and stir in fruit pectin. Continue stirring for 6 minutes, stopping to skim off the foam 2 or 3 times. Pour into hot, sterilized jars and cover with prepared lids and rims. When jars have cooled, check seal by ensuring lids are curved down slightly. Refrigerate jars after opening.

SAVOURY RICE

★ ★ ★

Serves 4

Serve this savoury rice hot with a main dish or chilled and pressed into individual food rings as an accompaniment to cold meats and salad.

1 ½ tbsp (22 mL) olive oil
2 eggs, lightly beaten
2 green onions, trimmed and thinly sliced
2 cups (500 mL) cooked long-grain rice, chilled
½ cup (125 mL) fresh or frozen peas
Salt and pepper

Heat oil in a large skillet over medium-high heat until hot, but not smoking.

Add egg and green onion and rapidly stir with a wooden spoon until just beginning to set.

Add the rice and peas and stir to combine.

When rice mixture is thoroughly heated, season with salt and pepper and serve.

FRENCH DRESSING

★ ★ ★

Makes ¾ cup (175 mL)

Make this traditional French dressing in advance and refrigerate to allow flavours to blend. Before serving, bring to room temperature and remove garlic pieces.

3 tbsp (45 mL) white wine vinegar
1 tsp (5 mL) Dijon mustard
Large pinch each granulated sugar, salt and pepper
⅓ cup (75 mL) olive oil
¼ cup (60 mL) vegetable oil
1 garlic clove, halved

In a medium bowl, whisk together vinegar, mustard, sugar, salt and pepper. Add oil in a steady stream and continue to whisk until vinaigrette is thick, creamy and well blended.

Remove to a jar; add garlic, cover and shake. Store in refrigerator and bring to room temperature before serving.

SALAD CREAM

★ ★ ★

Makes 1 cup (250 mL)

A specialty of British kitchens, salad cream was introduced commercially by the H. J. Heinz and Crosse and Blackwell companies after World War I, and it remains a favourite today as a salad dressing, sandwich spread or all-purpose dipping sauce.

2 egg yolks from precooked hard-boiled eggs
1 ½ tbsp (22 mL) white wine vinegar
2 tsp (10 mL) Dijon mustard
1 cup (250 mL) heavy cream (35% m.f.)
Pinch of cayenne pepper
1 tsp (5 mL) granulated sugar
Salt and white pepper

In a bowl, mash the egg yolks until broken down and creamy. Add the vinegar, mustard, cream, cayenne pepper and sugar and whisk until well blended.

If necessary, pass through a sieve to remove any small bits. Adjust seasoning with salt and white pepper; cover and refrigerate for 12 hours.

PARSNIP AND POTATO MASH

★ ★ ★

Serves 4 to 6

This vegetable combination goes well with many dishes and is a good alternative to serving mashed potatoes. Crème fraiche, an ingredient commonly found in European cooking, is difficult to obtain in North American markets. You will find our adapted recipe for crème fraiche on page 28.

1 lb (450 g) potatoes
1 lb (450 g) parsnips
2 tbsp (30 mL) crème fraiche (see page 28)
1 clove garlic, minced
½ tsp (2 mL) ground nutmeg
Salt and pepper

Peel potatoes and parsnips, removing the woody core from the parsnips. Cut both the potatoes and parsnips into medium-sized chunks.

Bring a large saucepan of salted water to a boil and add potatoes and parsnips. Return to a boil and cook, uncovered, until tender, about 10 to 15 minutes. Test for doneness by piercing vegetable with a fork; if cooked it will easily fall apart. Drain the vegetables and mash with a potato masher; keep warm.

In a small saucepan over medium-low heat, combine the crème fraiche, garlic and nutmeg. Cook 3 to 4 minutes, stirring frequently and taking care that it does not burn.

Stir infused crème fraiche into the mash to combine. Adjust seasoning with salt and pepper.

CREAMED CARROTS

★ ★ ★

Serves 4

This is an excellent way to present carrots. They taste delicious, and have a lively, bright colour, which enhances the presentation of your dish. Top with chopped chives or freshly milled black pepper.

1 lb (450 g) carrots, peeled and sliced in circles
1 in (2.5 cm) cinnamon stick
2 tbsp (30 mL) heavy cream (35% m.f.)
2 green onions, trimmed and finely sliced
½ tsp (2 mL) ground nutmeg
1 tbsp (15 mL) butter
½ tsp (2 mL) lemon juice
Salt and pepper

In a saucepan over medium heat, cook carrots with cinnamon stick in lightly salted water until soft.

Drain carrots and remove cinnamon stick. Mash carrots or pass them through a ricer until they are smooth. Reserve carrots in a warm bowl.

In a small saucepan over medium-low heat, combine cream and green onion and gently heat until scalding. Remove from heat and add cream mixture to carrots, bit by bit, until you reach the required texture of your mash.

Stir nutmeg, butter and lemon juice into carrot mash. Season with salt and pepper to taste.

BREAD SAUCE

★ ★ ★

Serves 4 to 6

This traditional British sauce recipe is typically served alongside roast meats or small game birds.

4 whole cloves
1 small onion, quartered
2 cups (500 mL) homogenized milk
1 bay leaf
6 peppercorns
½ tsp (2 mL) ground nutmeg
½ tsp (2 mL) salt
1 ½ cups (375 mL) white bread crumbs
1 tbsp (15 mL) butter
2 tbsp (30 mL) heavy cream (35% m.f.)
Salt and pepper

Stick a clove into each onion quarter.

In a saucepan, combine milk, clove-studded onion quarters, bay leaf, peppercorns, nutmeg and salt. Bring to just under the boiling point; remove from heat, cover and leave to infuse for 1 hour.

Using a slotted spoon, remove onion, cloves, peppercorns and bay leaf from milk. Return saucepan to medium heat; stir in bread crumbs and cook on a low simmer for 15 minutes, stirring occasionally.

Whisk butter and cream into sauce and adjust seasoning with salt and pepper to taste.

POULTRY STUFFING

★ ★ ★

Serves 6

This would make an excellent stuffing for the roast turkey that was served as a main course in the second-class dining room. This combination of good quality bread mixed with potato, celery, dried fruit and herbs produces a pleasing flavour that enhances but never overpowers the delicate taste of poultry.

2 tbsp (30 mL) olive oil
2 tbsp (30 mL) butter, plus extra for greasing
1 ½ cups (375 mL) diced celery
1 ½ cups (375 mL) diced onion
4 cups (1 L) day-old bread, torn into pieces
2 cups (500 mL) mashed potatoes
1 cup (250 mL) mixed dried fruit (a combination of apricots, apple, pear, cranberry, prune etc.)
1 tbsp (15 mL) dried sage (or to taste)
¼ to ½ cup (60 mL to 125 mL) chicken stock
Salt and pepper

Preheat oven to 350°F (180°C).

Heat olive oil and butter in a skillet over medium-low heat; add celery and onion and sauté until softened, about 8 minutes.

Remove onion and celery to a large bowl; add the bread, potato, mixed fruit and sage. Gently toss to combine. Add stock 2 tablespoons (30 mL) at a time, tossing the ingredients until stuffing is slightly moist.

Adjust seasoning with salt and pepper to taste.

Lightly spoon the dressing into a greased casserole dish and bake for 45 minutes, until heated through and lightly crisped on top.

POMMES PARMENTIER

★ ★ ★

Serves 4

Pommes Parmentier is basically cubed potatoes, sautéed and baked until they turn a lovely golden colour. Preparing potatoes in this way is very easy and makes an excellent accompaniment to many entrees.

4 tbsp (60 mL) olive oil
4 tbsp (60 mL) butter
2 lb (900 g) potatoes, peeled and cut in ¾ in (2 cm) cubes
1 small onion, chopped
1 clove garlic, minced
¼ cup (60 mL) dried breadcrumbs
Salt and pepper
½ lemon

Preheat oven to 400°F (200°C).

Heat oil and butter in a large ovenproof skillet over medium-high heat. Add cubed potato, onion and garlic and cook, stirring frequently, until the potatoes begin to brown, about 2 to 3 minutes.

Remove skillet to oven and bake, stirring occasionally, until cooked through and golden, about 30 minutes.

Remove potatoes to a serving bowl, gently stir in toasted bread crumbs and adjust seasoning with salt and pepper. Serve with a squeeze of lemon juice.

MANGO CHUTNEY

★ ★ ★

Makes 4 to 5 cups (1 to 1.5 L)

2 mangoes
2 apples
1 cup (250 mL) cider vinegar
1 ½ cups (375 mL) brown sugar
1 large onion, chopped
2 cloves garlic, minced
3 tbsp (45 mL) minced fresh ginger
½ tsp (2 mL) salt
½ cup (125 mL) golden raisins

Peel and medium-dice the mangoes and apples; reserve.

In a heavy saucepan, combine vinegar, sugar, onion, garlic, ginger and salt; bring to a boil over medium heat, stirring constantly. Stir in mango, apple and raisins and return to a boil. Reduce heat and simmer, uncovered, stirring occasionally, for 35 to 45 minutes or until desired consistency.

Ladle into hot, sterilized jars, leaving ½ inch (1.25 cm) headspace. Process jars in a hot water bath for 10 minutes.

MAYONNAISE

Makes 1 ½ cups (375 mL)

Bring all ingredients to room temperature before preparing.

Mayonnaise can be prepared using a food processor; substitute 1 whole egg for the egg yolk and add the vinegar between additions of the olive and vegetable oils. Processor mayonnaise will be lighter in colour.

1 large egg yolk
2 tsp (10 mL) Dijon mustard
⅔ cup (150 mL) olive oil
⅔ cup (150 mL) vegetable oil
2 tsp (10 mL) white wine vinegar or lemon juice
Salt and pepper

Using a deep bowl, whisk egg yolk and mustard until combined.

Whisk in the olive oil, a drop at a time, until the mixture begins to thicken. Whisking constantly, add the remaining oils in a slow, thin stream.

Still whisking constantly, add the vinegar a little at a time until the mayonnaise is emulsified. Adjust seasoning with salt and white pepper.

Store mayonnaise covered in the refrigerator and use within 3 to 4 days.

TURNIP PURÉE

Serves 4

Root vegetables would have been a staple vegetable in the early twentieth century. Turnip Purée was served in first- and second-class menus on the Titanic.

1 turnip, 1 ½ lbs (750 g)
1 tbsp (15 mL) brown sugar
½ cup (125 mL) heavy cream (35% m.f.)
2 tbsp (30 mL) butter, plus extra for greasing

Preheat oven to 350°F (200°C).

Peel and cube turnip. Boil in a saucepan until tender, about 25 to 35 minutes.

Drain turnip, sprinkle with sugar and mash until smooth. Stir in cream.

Place purée in a buttered casserole dish, dot with butter and bake 30 minutes.

CRUSTY ROLLS

★ ★ ★

Makes 2 dozen rolls

1 cup (250 mL) homogenized milk
¼ cup (60 mL) butter, plus extra for greasing
1 tsp (5 mL) salt
2 tbsp (30 mL) granulated sugar, divided
½ cup (125 mL) warm water
1 package or 2 ¼ tsp (11 mL) active dry yeast
1 egg
4 ½ cups (1.25 L) all-purpose flour

In a saucepan over medium heat, combine milk, butter, salt and 1 ½ tbsp (22 mL) of the sugar; heat until butter is melted. Remove from heat to slightly cool.

In a large bowl, dissolve remaining sugar in warm water. Sprinkle yeast over top and reserve in a warm place until frothy, about 10 minutes.

Add milk mixture and egg to the yeast and whisk to combine.

Stir in flour, 1 cup (250 mL) at a time, until it forms a soft dough. Turn out dough onto a lightly floured surface and knead, adding as much of the remaining flour as needed to prevent it from sticking. Continue kneading until the dough is elastic and smooth, about 10 minutes.

Place dough in a large greased bowl, turning it to grease all sides. Cover bowl and let dough rise in a warm place until doubled, about 1 ½ hours.

Punch down dough and remove to a lightly floured surface. Cut into 18 pieces. Stretch and pinch dough underneath, making the tops smooth and round.

Place a dough ball in the centre of 2 greased 9-inch (1.5 L) round baking pans. Surround the centre roll with 8 rolls. Cover and let rise in a warm place, 1 hour.

Bake in preheated 375ºF (190ºC) oven until rolls are golden and sound hollow when tapped on the bottom, about 25 to 30 minutes.

CUSTARD SAUCE

★ ★ ★

Serves 4, makes 3 cups (750 mL)

1 ¼ cups (310 mL) homogenized
  milk
1 ¼ cups (310 mL) heavy cream
  (35% m.f.)
4 in (10 cm) piece vanilla pod, split
  lengthways and seeded
6 egg yolks
⅓ cup (75 mL) granulated sugar

In top of a double boiler over simmering water, heat milk, cream, vanilla pod and seeds until scalding.

In a medium-large bowl, whisk egg yolks and sugar until pale and slightly thickened, about 2 to 3 minutes. Very gradually add cream mixture to egg mixture, stirring constantly until smooth.

Return mixture to double boiler and cook, stirring constantly, for 10 minutes or until thick enough to coat the back of a spoon.

Remove from heat and strain custard through a sieve to remove the vanilla bean and seeds. Pour custard into a warm jug for serving.

ACKNOWLEDGEMENTS

Roger Findlay, Boughton, Norfolk; Richard Stenlake, Scotland; the late Millvina Dean, Southampton; Judy Busch, California; Mark Solomon, Norfolk; Hilda and John Standen; Suffolk; Ena & Richard Proctor, California; Diana & Bill Beeson, Norfolk; Leanne & James Dewart, Norfolk; Barrie Carson Turner, Norfolk.

Yvonne

We would like to thank the wonderful staff and management at the Hart & Thistle Gastropub in Halifax for preparing and styling the recipes in this book. We would also like to thank Jen Partridge for bringing the dishes to life with her fantastic photography.

Elaine and Virginia

PHOTO CREDITS

l=left, r=right, t=top, b=bottom, c=centre

All interior photos by Jen Partridge of Partridge Photography, except where noted below:

istock photography: 4, 6b, 12, 19t, 20t, 21t, 29, 33, 45, 63, 68, 82, 83, 84, 86, 88, 90, 92, 93; Nova Scotia Archives: 1, 6t, 8t, 10t, 10c; Roger Findlay: 18, 19 (except t), 20 (except t), 21 (except t), 47, 62, 73, 80, 89; Titanic Museum Attractions, Branson, MO and Pigeon Forge, TN, USA: 10b

INDEX